Brachiosaurus

Daniel Nunn

Raintree is an imprint of Capstone Global Library Limited, a company incorporated in England and Wales having its registered office at 7 Pilgrim Street, London, EC4V 6LB – Registered company number: 6695582

www.raintreepublishers.co.uk
myorders@raintreepublishers.co.uk

Text © Capstone Global Library Limited 2015
First published in paperback in 2016
The moral rights of the proprietor have been asserted.

Edited by Daniel Nunn and James Benefield
Designed by Tim Bond
Picture research by Tracy Cummins
Production by Helen McCreath
Originated by Capstone Global Library Ltd
Printed and bound in China

ISBN 978 1 4062 8084 5 (hardback)
18 17 16 15 14
10 9 8 7 6 5 4 3 2 1

ISBN 978 1 4062 8091 3 (paperback)
19 18 17 16 15
10 9 8 7 6 5 4 3 2

British Library Cataloguing in Publication Data
A full catalogue record for this book is available from the British Library.

Acknowledgements
We would like to thank the following for permission to reproduce photographs: Alamy p. 11 (© Christian Darkin); Corbis pp. 14, 15 (© Jim Zuckerman); Getty Images pp. 18, 23 (Ulrich Baumgarten), 19 (Ken Lucas), 20 (Gamma-Rapho); Science Source pp. 6, 8 right (Roger Harris); Shutterstock pp. 4, 7, 10, 13 (Kostyantyn Ivanyshen), 5b (Audrey Snider-Bell), 5c (KAMONRAT), 5d (tratong), 8 left (James Steidl), 9 left (Bob Orsillo), 9 right (Hector Conesa), 9 scale (seesaw), 16 (Dereje), 23 (tratong); Superstock pp. 5a (Science Photo Library), 12 (imagebroker.net), 17 (Stocktrek Images), 21 (Louie Psihoyos).

Cover photograph of an adult brachiosaurus altithorax on a beach in what is today North America, reproduced with permission of Superstock (NHPA).

Back cover photograph of Brachiosaurus reprodcued with permission of Shutterstock (Kostyantyn Ivanyshen).

We would like to thank Dee Reid and Nancy Harris for their invaluable help in the preparation of this book.

Every effort has been made to contact copyright holders of material reproduced in this book. Any omissions will be rectified in subsequent printings if notice is given to the publisher.

Contents

Meet Brachiosaurus

Brachiosaurus was a dinosaur.
Dinosaurs lived long ago.

dinosaur

crocodile

lizard

snake

Dinosaurs were reptiles.
Crocodiles, snakes and lizards
are reptiles that live today.

What was Brachiosaurus like?

Brachiosaurus was a very big dinosaur.

Brachiosaurus had long legs.

Brachiosaurus was as tall as
a building with four floors!

Brachiosaurus was as heavy as 12 elephants!

tail

Brachiosaurus had a tail.

Brachiosaurus
had a very
long neck.

Brachiosaurus had a small head.

Brachiosaurus ate plants.

Brachiosaurus
had to eat
all day to get
enough food!

Brachiosaurus may have lived
for 100 years!

Where is Brachiosaurus now?

Brachiosaurus is extinct. There are no Brachiosaurus alive now.

All the dinosaurs died long ago.

We learn about Brachiosaurus from fossils.

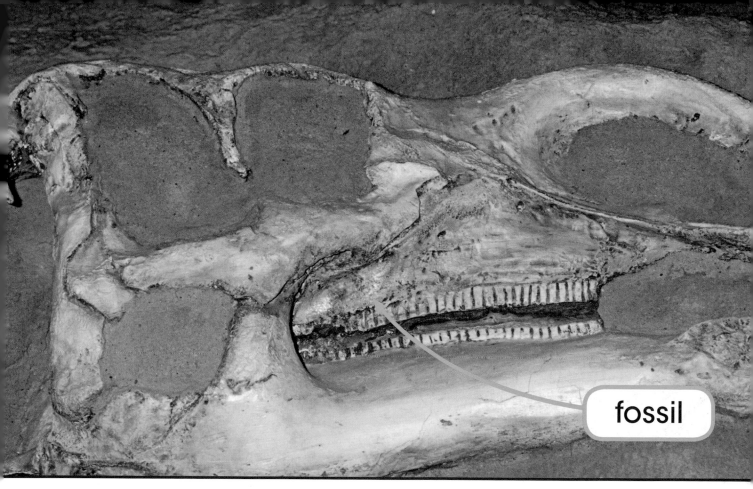

fossil

Fossils are animal bones that
have turned to rock.

People find fossils in the ground.

Fossils show us what Brachiosaurus looked like.

Where in the world?

Brachiosaurus fossils have been found in North America, Europe and Africa.

Picture glossary

 **fossil** animal bones or parts of a plant that have turned into rock

 **reptile** cold-blooded animal. A lizard is a reptile.

How to say it

Brachiosaurus: say 'brack-ee-uh-sawr-us'

Index

Notes for parents and teachers

Before reading

Ask the children to name some dinosaurs. Ask them if dinosaurs are around today. Talk about how some dinosaurs ate plants and others ate other dinosaurs. Can they think of ways these dinosaurs might have been different? Have they heard of Brachiosaurus? Find out if they already know anything about this dinosaur.

After reading

- Ask the children if they remember what a Brachiosaurus looked like – talk about its long neck and other physical characteristics. Make a Brachiosaurus collage together.
- Draw a four-storey building and get the children to stick on bricks and windows. Then ask the children to guide you as you draw a picture of a Brachiosaurus next to the building. Now the children can stick on green and brown materials to decorate the Brachiosaurus.